The **Price** of **Financial Freedom**

Niyi Adeoshun

The **Price** of **Financial Freedom**

3 Essential Steps For Breaking the Cycle of Debt

Nukan Publishing

"For anything worth having, one must pay the price; and the price is always work, patience, love, self-sacrifice - no paper currency, no promises to pay, but the gold of real service."
-- John Burroughs

"For which of you, intending to build a tower, does not sit down first and count the cost, whether he has enough to finish it?"
-- Luke 14:28

"Incredible change happens in your life when you decide to take control of what you do have power over instead of craving control over what you don't."
-- Steve Maraboli

The Price of Financial Freedom
(3 Essential Steps For Breaking the Cycle of Debt)
by Niyi Adeoshun
Copyright © 2017, 2022 Niyi Adeoshun

http://www.niyiadeoshun.com

Published by: Nukan Publishing
ISBN: 979-8440658028

First Edition: 2017
Second Edition: 2022

Cover-design by: Adaku Oppong-Manu

Notice of Rights
All rights reserved. No part of this book may be reproduced in any form or by any electronic or mechanical means including information storage and retrieval systems, without permission in writing from the author. The only exception is by a reviewer, who may quote short excerpts in a review. For information on getting permission for reprints and excerpts, contact admin@nukan.com

Notice of Liabilities

The Publisher has strived to be as accurate and complete as possible in the creation of this book, notwithstanding the fact that he does not warrant or represent at any time that the contents within are accurate due to the rapidly changing nature of the financial world.

While all attempts have been made to verify information provided in this publication, the Publisher assumes no responsibility for errors, omissions, or contrary interpretation of the subject matter herein. Any perceived slights of specific persons, peoples, or organisations are unintentional.

This book is not intended for use as a source of legal, business, accounting or financial advice. All readers are advised to seek services of competent professionals in legal, business, accounting, and finance fields.

Copyright Notices

All Scriptures used in this book are taken from the New King James Version (NKJV) unless otherwise indicated.

King James Version (KJV) is in the public domain.

Scripture taken from the New King James Version®. Copyright © 1982 by Thomas Nelson, Inc.
Used by permission. All rights reserved.

Scripture quotations marked NLT are taken from the Holy Bible, New Living Translation copyright© 1996, 2004, 2007 by Tyndale House Foundation.
Used by permission of Tyndale House Publishers, Inc. Carol Stream, Illinois 60188. All rights reserved.

Scriptures marked AMP are taken from the AMPLIFIED BIBLE (AMP): Scripture taken from the AMPLIFIED® BIBLE, Copyright © 1954, 1958, 1962, 1964, 1965, 1987 by the Lockman Foundation Used by Permission. (www.Lockman.org)

What Others Are Saying ....

What a piece!

As a psychiatrist and a strong believer in the efficacy of the Word of God, I admire Niyi's approach in this book. He has a balanced blend of biblical principles on how to bring about financial freedom. Your thoughts and your words influence your choices, attitudes and behaviour. Niyi has drawn in a wealth of knowledge in this book. It is highly recommended.

Dr Joyce Edeki
Consultant Psychiatrist,
Kent. UK

This is a book for everyone — from those who are financially savvy to those who rely on all incomes in their household to survive each month. I say this because, no matter the place you are in life, no one is ever too rich or too deep in debt to be encouraged about taking steps for a better tomorrow.

This book reminded me that the financial freedom I desire for myself and my family is a journey that has no end. It isn't something you save up for and purchase as a one off. It is a mind-set, a continuous sacrifice and lifelong change to be enjoyed by my family and generations to come.

Palangfat Adeshipe
Sophia Karis Events, UK

This book is one of the most challenging and positive books I have read in years. It is so straight to the point and addresses most things that we do daily and often overlook, thinking we have it all in hand. Niyi has so much challenged me that I am now setting myself out to becoming financially-free.

This is the first book that I have read at a sitting; I just could not put it down as I wanted to learn more and more. I would recommend this book to anyone, everyone, who wants to live in freedom. I loved it. Refreshing.

Anthony Olomofe,
Youth Project Leader, Basildon, UK

The Price of Financial Freedom is a book anyone serious about being financially-free should read. The book is written in a clear, concise and encouraging manner and will no doubt propel you forward to begin your journey on the path to financial freedom.

Femi Magbagbeola
IT Consultant, London, UK

This book is packed with powerful thoughts and advice; delivered through simple stories that can enable anyone to learn a lot from it.

Niyi has written the book in a manner to generate a deep thinking process for all by maintaining the simplicity of the language throughout the book for example, "*If you are casual about your freedom, you will become a casualty*". In this regard, the book will perfectly serve the purpose of infusing positive thoughts of becoming debt free. I strongly recommend this book. Don't miss out!

Tolu Omoleigho
Director, Oak Management Services Ltd,
Kent UK

Dedication

There are those who just dream …

but …

… there are those who believe that by faith, hard work, determination, dedication and self-discipline, they can turn those dreams into reality.

This book is dedicated to you.

All things are possible to those who believe.

Acknowledgement

This book could not have been written to its fullest and best without the help of many people in their own unique ways.

Firstly, I want to thank Efua Quartey-Ochu, Ruth Oyelakin and Victoria Ezeagbo for brainstorming with me in working through the book's title and its subtitle.

Words alone cannot express my gratitude to my friends, Femi and Tokunbo Magbagbeola, for their advice and assistance in polishing this manuscript right from its initial stages.

Special thanks to my long-time friend and fellow author, Eruvwu Obuaya, for taking the time to provide the foreword for this book and to the reviewers Tolu Omoleigho, Anthony Olomofe, Dr Joyce Edeki and Palangfat Adeshipe, who allowed their opinions of the finished product to be made public.

For understanding my long days (and nights) at the computer, I'd like to thank the love of my life, my wife,

Joyce, and our sons, Vince, Chris and David for their ever-constant support.

Finally, I give thanks to the Lord God Almighty, the Giver of life and of second chances – without Whom this book could never have become a reality.

Table of Contents

What Others Are Saying ix

Dedication xiii

Acknowledgement xv

Foreword xix

Introduction xxi

Chapter 1: What Is Financial Freedom? 25

Chapter 2: The Need For Financial Freedom 31

Chapter 3: The Price of Thought-Change 43

Chapter 4: The Price of Speech-Change 65

Chapter 5: The Price of Facing Oppositions 81

Chapter 6: Learn to Play the Game of Life 91

Chapter 7: The Prize of Change 99

Chapter 8: And Finally 105

Financial Freedom Series 111

About The Author 112

Other Books by the Author 113

Resources 114

Foreword

Financial independence for all is a passion of mine, and that has been the case for many years. I am a firm believer in the fact that it is the parents' responsibility to leave an inheritance to their children's children, as the Bible has said, but how can they do that if they themselves are not financially free first?

So, I read this book with interest and can truly say that everyone starting on the journey to financial freedom should read it.

Think about it – the opposite of freedom is slavery or bondage. So if you are not financially free, you might be in bondage of some kind. Bondage to your job or your bank, etc. Slaves are usually not *just* set free; someone has got to pay a price. For YOUR financial freedom, YOU have to pay that price!

If you're struggling in your bid to become financially free, you should definitely read this book, especially if you're a parent and live from paycheque to paycheque.

This is your opportunity to get up and show your offspring a different way of living.

Why?

The Price of Financial Freedom gives you insights into financial freedom that you probably didn't know about or haven't yet implemented. Niyi, whom I have known for many years, provides you with tips and suggestions that, if utilised, will help you become financially free or at least set you on the right path towards it.

This well-written and easy-to-read book should be treated as a guide to help you on your way to financial freedom. The author's years of experience and training is indeed worth your time, so grab a cup of coffee (or your personal favourite beverage) and don't put this book down until you're done reading it!

Eruvwu Joyce Obuaya
Author of "Anchored Assurance"
Entrepreneur, Surrey, UK

Introduction

As with anything that is worth having, financial freedom does not happen by accident; it happens by design and by taking deliberate actions. Making it happen requires clear decisions, determination, discipline and motivation mixed with appropriate and timely actions.

Of course, there is a price to be paid in order to go from your initial decision to your desired result; and that is exactly what this book is about.

Mind you, not everyone wants to worry about paying any price for financial freedom. Some people are very comfortable with the way they (and the things around them) are. They think they are better off just *letting the sleeping dogs lie*. They already know that the first step is the most difficult and that feathers are going to be ruffled if they ever take that step. Thus, they do nothing, achieve nothing, stay the same or get even worse financially.

On the other hand, there are those people who, not liking certain aspects of their lives – especially their finances, have decided that something must be done and have also decided to take complete responsibility for their own financial future. If that is you, then you are on the right track and in the right place by reading this book.

History has shown numerous times that anyone and everyone who has made the decision to become financially successful has the potential to be able to do it - **as long as they are willing to pay the price.**

You only get out of life according to what you have put in. If you want more, put in more.

At the end of the day, everyone needs to be able to look himself or herself in the mirror and ask these simple questions:

- Am I where I wish to be financially – at this point in my life?
- If not, where do I actually desire to be?
- What do I need to do to get there?
- Am I willing to do whatever is necessary to move my finances forward?

This book, **"The Price of Financial Freedom"**, will help you answer these questions and more – just read on.

I wish you success,

Niyi Adeoshun
Money Management Coach

Chapter 1
What Is Financial Freedom?

I believe I will be able to define financial freedom better if I define *freedom* first.

At any point in time, there always seems to be one conflict or another in a corner of the world. People are fighting for freedom or rights; press freedom, religious freedom, political freedom, sexual freedom, etc. Even politicians, sports & movie stars seek privacy (or personal freedom) during the times they are not on the field, track, and stage or in office.

Every human being on earth seeks freedom. However, freedom is defined in different ways by different people under different conditions. Freedom means something very different to those who have only known tyranny, as compared to those who have not. For those who have lived in bondage, no price is too high to pay for freedom, while for those who have never experienced subjugation, this kind of freedom often has little meaning.

It is strange, however, that some people who are in servitude don't even realise that they are! Others, who do, act as though their freedom would just be thrown into their laps without them lifting a finger.

Having freedom always comes with a price tag in one way or another, and in no other situation is that statement truer than in financial freedom.

What Is Financial Freedom?

The fact that it contains the word "financial" does not mean that financial freedom is only about money. You will not get the money if you do not add other necessary things to your life; freedom cannot be compartmentalised.

Financial freedom is not the same as being rich - although people often confuse the two. One person earning £30,000 per annum could be completely financially free while another is still financially strapped even though he has a £300,000 annual income.

What Is Financial Freedom?

Ask an average person on the streets what financial freedom is and you will hear something like *"When I win the lottery, I'll be financially free"*, *"If my parents leave me a huge inheritance, then my money problems will be over"*. This kind of thinking indicates two mistakes that people are making about financial freedom.

- Firstly, that being financially free can only be reached by those with a large amount of cash, thus immediately counting themselves and many others out.

- Secondly, that financial freedom is all about money – and they may not have enough to reach that stage.

Financial planners will tell you that people tend to overestimate the amount they really need to achieve financial freedom. You can actually calculate the necessary amount with reasonable accuracy using details of your monthly income (from all sources) and your monthly expenses.

Huge amounts of money being dumped on you without proper financial education does not make one financially free; just look at the lottery winners who have ended back in the 'poor house' after just a few years of mindless spending.

****

"Quick riches are often more dangerous than poverty"
— Napoleon Hill

****

Financial freedom is the state of having sufficient personal wealth to live on indefinitely without having to actively work to cover your basic necessities. At this stage you would have enough passive income generated by your assets to cover your monthly expenses. For example, a person's monthly expenses may total £2,500, but his income received passively from shares, dividends, rental properties, businesses, etc. averages about £3,000 a month; this person can be deemed to be financially free.

Wouldn't you like that?

I bet you would!

When you are financially free, you would:

- Work for money because you CHOOSE to, not because you HAVE to.

What Is Financial Freedom?

- Be free from the stress and strain of wondering how you will manage to pay your fixed monthly expenses.

- Support yourself (as well as dependents) financially and conveniently without being forced to take on any undesirable job just to earn an income.

- Have the freedom to be who you really are, be what you have been created to be and fulfil your real purpose in life.

One question I have often been asked is, **"I know you said financial freedom is the way to go, with its benefits and all, but is it necessary for everyone?"**

Read on: The next chapter will reveal the answer to that question.

Chapter 2
The Need For Financial Freedom

Did you know that you will still need about 70% of your current income to live on in retirement as you do today?

I hope that has not come as a shock to you.

Of course, that means your home, cars, and everything else should have been paid off by that time. If not, trouble is on the horizon, and you have to begin addressing your financial situation right away.

Financial planners reckon that by the age of 65, you should have put away £25 for every £1 you expect to spend annually from your savings or pension during retirement. The assumption is that, all things being equal, it is possible you will live on to be 90 years old even though you have retired at 65! To be more accurate, you need to take an inflation rate of, at least, 3% into consideration as well when calculating retirement funds. This means that whatever costs you

The Price of Financial Freedom

£50,000 today will cost £67,195 in 10 years' time and about £90,305 in 20 years' time!

You see, it is either that many people don't know (or understand) these facts, or they don't care enough to respond positively to the information; while some others still think their governments will take care of them in retirement! Dream on!!

Let me create a scenario that will bring my point closer to home:

Imagine you get to work one morning only to be told that it is the last day of business for your company because the firm has suddenly fallen into financial difficulties; it can no longer sustain its operations and has been declared *insolvent*. How would you feel? Or what if you are just "let go" because the company is *undergoing restructuring?* What would be your reaction to such news?

Honestly speaking, as an average person, you would be scared and worried at the news because you may not have enough savings to sustain you until you find another job, or worse, you are in so much debt that you cannot afford to be unemployed even for one day! So, in that case, you are in trouble no matter how high your salary is or used to be.

Statistics reveal that the life savings of an average 50-year-old, in developed countries, is about £3200! You (and your family) cannot last two months on this amount of money. Worse still, with almost 100% of disposable income now being taken up by debt repayment, any hiccup in your employment, no matter how short, could create dire financial consequences for people.

These examples above should have been enough to convince anyone that financial freedom is necessary, but it is a known fact that we human beings love *taking the easy way out* of situations even if it is not the best way. We naturally follow the path of least resistance; we will try to get something for nothing (*or eat our cakes and still have it*) - if possible. Unless something is deemed very important, we usually do nothing about it.

The story below might illustrate what I mean:

> *A young couple on holiday walked past a house where an elderly man and his wife were lounging on their porch. Lying in between them*

was their dog, which was moaning and groaning. This scenario was repeated over several days, each time the younger couple passed this family. These curious, animal-loving holidaymakers decided that if the same thing happened again the following day, they would ask the family about the dog in distress.

Sure enough, the next day, it was the same scene exactly when they walked past the house. So they stopped and asked the elderly couple, "What is wrong with your dog?"

The elderly lady replied, "There is nothing wrong with him; he is just lying on a board that has a nail sticking up." The tourists then asked why the dog wouldn't just get up and lie somewhere else. They were told **"the nail bothers him enough to make him moan and groan, but it's not hurting him badly enough to make him get up and move".**

Would you agree with me that this is how some of us live our lives? People just keep complaining about the things they don't like - jobs, relationships, finances, their whole lives ... without getting up and doing something about them.

So if financial freedom is so necessary and even desirable to all, why isn't everybody aiming for it?

I can give you a few reasons:

- People want it...but they don't want to work for it.
- They want it...but they don't want to invest anything to get it.
- They want it...but they don't want to risk anything for it.
- They want it...but they don't want to pay the price for it.
- They want the freedom...but they don't get it because they want it to be free!

By not choosing freedom, they have chosen **bondage** - by default.

Freedom Is a Choice

We make hundreds of choices every day through our thoughts, words and actions. What we do with our money are choices and they will bring us satisfaction or regrets because *every choice is a seed and the result is the harvest*. With every choice we make, we risk being right or wrong depending on the information we possessed beforehand.

So what is a risk?

Risk, according to the dictionary, is the potential that a chosen action or activity (including the choice of inaction) will lead to a loss or an undesirable outcome. It is the exposure to the possibility of loss, injury, or other adverse or unwelcome circumstance; a chance or situation involving such a possibility.

Every one of our pursuits in life has a risk - with different degrees of intensity. Every choice we make carries an element of risk. Waking up in the morning and choosing to get out of bed carries the risk of you FALLING out of bed - just to begin with.

Look around you; everything we do in life stems from the choices we make daily — each with its own risk.

However, don't allow the risk, the fear of failure or the attractiveness of *playing it safe* in life to stop you from achieving your freedom. I am not advising you to be reckless with your life, but those who have become financially free know that life is about taking <u>calculated</u> risks with every decision.

****

"Most people fail in life not because they aim too high and miss but because they aim too low and hit"
- Les Brown

****

Can you score a goal if you take a penalty kick in a football match? You don't know because you have not tried it yet. You have to commit yourself first without thinking of failure because you will not know what you can do unless you try. It is not what you don't have, but the things you think you need that keep you from being successful.

Real financial freedom requires individual risk-taking toward becoming a winner. Those who have experienced success in anything have also experienced failure at some points on their journeys. In order to pursue success, one must accept the risk of failure, and in order to succeed, one must endure and overcome those failures.

****

"In order to succeed, your desire for success should be greater than your fear of failure."
- William Cosby

****

Every Choice Is a Sacrifice

We all have comfort zones, which are cosy and enjoyable. You don't stress or strain there, but at the same time, you may just be floating downstream like a dead fish. There, you have no pain but get no gain; you have no price to pay and thus no prize to receive.

Many of the things you desire in life are always waiting for you just outside your comfort zone. To gain your freedom financially or otherwise, you have to stretch yourself. Every choice is a sacrifice. Whenever you make a choice, you are embracing one thing at the expense of the other. You must sacrifice mediocrity to gain excellence, just as you must sacrifice *comfortable* bondage in debt for financial freedom.

****

"There are two primary choices in life: to accept conditions as they exist, or accept the responsibility for changing them."
- Denis Waitley

****

It is one thing to set goals, but quite another to achieve them. When it comes to setting goals, many people think it is about making wishes, hoping they will come true. So they make a wish list, label the items goals and go after them half-heartedly without the commitment to pay the full price. When *push comes to shove*, they pull back and return to their comfort zone, with excuses to justify why they failed to reach their targets.

Wishes are easily identified - "I wish"; dreams appear in the form of "I want", but goals appear in the form of "I will" - your willingness to pay the price is necessary for achieving anything or reaching any goal.

The 'Can-Do' Spirit

Nothing is impossible to you if you have *faith*. If anyone has ever achieved what you want to achieve, then it is possible. The fact that no one around you has ever been financially free does not mean YOU cannot do it. Napoleon Hill said, *"Whatever the mind can conceive and believe, it can achieve"*. George Bernard Shaw, in his own wise way, said, *"Some men see things as they are and ask why. Others dream things that never were and ask why not"*.

The common belief, in athletics, up to May 1954, was that a human being could not run the Mile in under 4 minutes without his heart exploding – that was until Roger Bannister did it. In the next 12 months, close to one hundred other athletes achieved that same feat – some even improved on that record time. What changed? Nothing but mind-set, and Roger Bannister's 'Can-Do' spirit that flung the gates of possibility open for all. People now know that running a mile in under 4 minutes can be done.

It is common knowledge that human beings don't even attempt things that they don't believe can be done. Financial freedom is possible; so position yourself as that person who steps out to pay the full price to achieve his or her freedom and encourages others to do the same. What is unrealistic and unreasonable is attempting to obtain this freedom by paying half the price. *If you are casual about your freedom, you will become a casualty of a life in bondage.*

In this life, there are no freebies, discounts or "buy-now, pay later". You have to pay the full price upfront before you can obtain your freedom. We all have to follow due process to gain this financial freedom; there are no shortcuts. Financial freedom is achievable. Your ability to achieve freedom is determined by your willingness to pay the price in full. The bigger the price you are willing to pay, the bigger the reward you can receive. Mind you, freedom is a privilege, but it is also a big responsibility

- Are you willing to pay the price – in full?
- Are you willing to give it all it takes to achieve your financial freedom?
- Are you willing to become what you've never been in order to have what you've never had before?

The Price of Financial Freedom

If you have answered 'Yes' to any of the questions above, the next question is: **What price do you actually have to pay to achieve financial freedom?**

Chapter 3
The Price of Thought-Change

The first price you have to pay for your financial freedom is to consciously make a change in how you think about yourself and your circumstances.

Observe your surroundings for a moment; everything you see began as a thought or an idea in someone's mind. The more intense a thought is, the more powerful its manifestation will be.

Just like you are what you eat, it also follows that you are (or become) what you think about. In other words, the way you think creates your world. Do you like everything you see in YOUR world without the need for any improvement? If 'Yes', then you can put this book down right now and go on your merry way – there's no need to change anything. But if your answer is 'Not So Much' or a blatant 'No', then it is time to change what you think about and how you think about them.

****

"You become what you think about most of the time"
- *Jim Rohn*

****

The favourite pastime of the mind is *being right* all the time; that is, until it receives better or alternative information. You have to discover what is right for you (your desire) and impress that new information on your mind so it can have something new to work on.

If you have set your mind to work for somebody as an employee, you will look for a job, and you will be satisfied working as an employee. However, if you set your mind to attain financial freedom, you will find other exclusive or additional means of getting wealthy without the pressures and hassles of working for someone else for the rest of your life.

Sometimes, when I tell folks about additional income streams, they go out and get a second job! That is good only if that job is for a specific period and for a specific purpose. In a second job, you will pay more taxes, and you will still not be in control of your money and your time! What I'm talking about is you starting something, no matter how small, which can continue to pay you profits even when you're no longer *slaving* in it. As Jim Rohn puts it: **"Profits are better than wages"**. He also said, **"Wages make you a living, but profits make you a fortune"**. In your new ventures, profits may come out in trickles at the beginning, but in the long run, they can turn out to be the streams that will feed your wealth pool for years to come. Think about that!

Working for a salary only has not yet and may never make anyone wealthy. Your becoming wealthy is not your employer's responsibility, it is yours! Invest in yourself outside of office hours. Find other ways to increase your income in addition to your salary; then think of ways to make that income big enough to replace your current salary. Your employers can determine your *wages,* but only you can determine your *income.*

Your wealth building stems from what you do AFTER you have done what you are required to do on a daily basis. Going above the call of duty develops excellence in you. Use that same excellence to create other sources of income for yourself.

It seems that the minds of most people have been so conditioned to working as employees that they forget, unintentionally ignore or fail to see how they can create real wealth for themselves by seeking additional sources of income. Just like on a coin, they are so used to one side that they never bothered to look and to find out what it feels like to be on the other side of it. They become so used to being the '*tail*' that they don't want to acknowledge that there is a '*head*' just a flip away.

Do you realise that the word "job" fits as an acronym for "**J**ust **O**ver **B**roke?" Having a job (as an employee) allows you to earn just enough to cover your daily expenses – if you can budget well. If you lose your job, you're broke – unless you have an emergency fund or some other savings to cushion the blow. Having a job or working as an employee for someone else means your privileges are limited and confined. A job basically pays you for the position you occupy in the company, not for your worth as a person. If you want something different, today is the day to begin.

Although your salary may be 'guaranteed', it is also limited. You see, employers pay just enough so that employees don't quit. Consequently, some employees work hard enough just so they don't get fired. Subconsciously, however, if you are an employee today and you stick to that 'just enough' mentality, the creative side of your mind will not have the chance to work at its full capacity. Your full creativity is needed in your job as well as in your business, or else you may be making somebody rich, but definitely that somebody is not you, not financially or intellectually.

As *just* an employee, you give up control of your finances to somebody else, and you are automatically at their mercy. If your employer's business slows down or fails completely, you will go down with it, but if it prospers, you don't necessarily get to share in the profits. The only consolation is – you get to keep your job. Most likely, you stay where you are and on the same salary. To surrender one's finances to somebody else is like having your future in somebody else's hands, and you can't do anything about it.

****

"Build your own dreams, or someone else will hire you to build theirs."
- Farrah Gray

****

I'm not saying that being an employee is bad – no, not at all. I have been in several jobs in my adult life, and the salaries from them have helped me and my family to live a good life. Employers provide jobs, which is good for the economy of any nation. I'm only painting a picture (as brutal as it may seem) of one of life's realities, which goes unnoticed; in order to activate (or re-activate) the financial intelligence region of your mind.

I once heard the story of a Bus Driver who put his children through schools, colleges and University - even medical schools without debt and on his average salary. "How did he do it?", you may be asking. You see, with lots of time on his hands in between journeys and while others were drinking coffee and reading newspapers, this man used his time to study *(and learn from)* top investors, their habits and their good investments early in life. He spent his money wisely, invested with knowledge and retired with a $3million investment portfolio! A Bus Driver!!

Consider this for a moment: The open palm of a hand facing up is receiving, but when facing down, it is giving. In the same way, employees receive money after they have worked of course, whilst employers give. How do you want your palm's position to be in 10 years' time? Still receiving from your employers only or from YOUR other clients and investments also? Henry Ford said, *"It is not the employer who pays the wages. Employers only handle the money. It is the customer who pays the wages."* While your company may have many clients, you (the employee) have only one client – your employers. Serve them well! If you want to get paid more, serve more clients or create more sources of income.

Using the same *open-palm* analogy, lenders give and borrowers receive, but that usually **happens only once** during the period of a loan agreement. After the borrower has received the loan, the giving or receiving roles are reversed; the borrower continues to give while the lender keeps on receiving until the loan (plus the interest) is paid off. The borrower cannot afford to be sick or be laid off from work, and even though he/she is working hard, he or she will not be seeing the fruits of his/her labour until the loan is paid-off. In such a situation, the borrower is in what is referred to as the 'Rat Race'.

Wealth and Income

The fact that you are reading this book shows that you are ready to cross the dividing line between being a slave to money and being a master of it. It shows you are interested in creating wealth - an all-important factor to financial freedom.

Allow me to mention here that *wealth* is not the same as *income*. You can have a huge income and not be wealthy, just as you can be wealthy but have an average income. Income is received while wealth is created, built or accumulated. However, your income is your most powerful wealth-building tool. Remember that.

There are so many issues that underline the accumulation of wealth. To accumulate wealth, you must first spend less than you make and then save the rest. That is just the beginning of wealth building. How the money you have saved increases depends on the investments you make. In any case, you must have the initial 'seed' money to begin with, which can be quite difficult when you are in debt and in the 'rat race'.

What Does The "Rat Race" Mean?

Picture this: Every morning, you get up and prepare yourself to go to work - shower, eat breakfast, get dressed, travel to work by taxi/bus/train or drive your car, work from nine to five, return home to have dinner, watch television or read the newspapers, then off to bed you go till the next morning when the process starts all over again.

You get two to four weeks' paid leave each year and, without fail, get paid by your employer for your services every payday. If you decide you don't like your job anymore, you find another employer for better pay. Year in, year out, it's the same routine. You work for someone else, not for yourself; you become focused on making someone else richer using your strength, getting older, thinking of how to change things, but can't seem to find a way out of the rot. That is the "rat race."

Let me ask you: If you have ever been an employee or if you are still one, honestly, do you truly like this 'rat race' feeling?

I believe you'll agree with me that, as *just* an employee, your world is confined and limited to certain (and specific) information only. You hardly have time for other activities or to learn anything new. This limits your knowledge or potential, virtually crippling your mind.

Another disadvantage you get for being *just* an employee is that your income is forever limited. An average employee earning an average salary could hardly put aside a certain amount of money for savings for his or her future use. Even an above-average employee who could put aside some savings would hardly have enough for retirement. It is even pointless to try and calculate the savings of below-average employees, as they would be considered lucky if they don't become debt-ridden.

All too often, people are so trapped in this "rat race" that they never bother to know where life is leading them. They only notice it at times when they run short of cash for unexpected expenses or when they occasionally think of what will happen to them as they approach their retirement age, but mostly forget about it after some time and continue to do nothing to improve their lives.

The Price of Thought-Change

You must realise the need to get out of the "rat race" as early as possible. To achieve this, you need to change your way of thinking - from working as *just* an employee for someone else, to being in *control of your own time and money.*

I don't know what activities you partake in on a regular basis, but the following questions can get your brainstorming juices going:

- What are your hobbies?
- What experiences do you have?
- What resources are available to you?
- Which of the above can be developed into an income-generating product or service?

I'm not saying you should quit your day job right away, but you could spend some of your free time learning and actually implementing moneymaking activities while still working as an employee. Profis from these may help you become debt-free first. Once you are in control of your finances again and have enough knowledge on (and experience in) acquiring wealth AND your extra income is comparable to your current wages, that's the time to get out of the "rat race" and start living your new life while continuing to build your wealth at a faster rate.

Once out of the "rat race," you should aim to continue to work; only this time, you work for yourself and not just for other people. When you work for yourself, it does not mean that you're being selfish; you're just being smart. Remember that when you begin working for yourself, you will still be working with people, so don't burn bridges behind you.

The bottom line is this: it is alright to be an employee, but just don't stay as one without creating additional sources of income as you go along. I'm talking from experience. Nobody's going to look after your financial life except you. Do something about it now!

What Information Do You Hold On Personal Finance?

Nothing changes your mind like new information that agrees with your new mindset. How much knowledge do you have about becoming financially free? You need knowledge, but not just any kind; you need a special kind of information to get you to where you want to be.

The Price of Thought-Change

Try to spend about one hour each day reading books on personal finance (the one you're reading now included). Getting good information will at least help you keep watch on your income and outgoings in a better way. Be warned, however, that the world will not pay you for what you know, but it can only pay you for what you DO with what you know. Reading alone will not *cut it*. Practice what you've learnt at the earliest opportunity.

Applied Knowledge Is Power.

Take driving a car, for example; it doesn't matter how much you 'know' about driving a car, until you actually get behind the steering wheel and drive successfully, you never really know; and so it is with everything else in life.

Put the budgeting, money-making, saving and investing information to practice as soon as you get the chance to do so. You must, however, learn to sift through this new information and use only those that agree with your situation and your new mindset.

For many people, there is usually a gap between their financial *knowing* and *doing*. That is the time lag between when they know what they should be doing and when they actually start doing it. The Bible says in Proverbs 21:20 that **"There is desirable treasure, and oil in the dwelling of the wise, but a foolish man squanders it."** While there are others, this verse just mentions one thing that differentiates the wise from the foolish - the wise save but, the unwise do not. Another one is: The wise don't have a knowing-to-doing gap; they just go ahead and pay the price now because they know there's a reward coming later.

Being wise is not the same as being educated or being a degree-holder; there are lots of foolish, educated people walking around. In the same vein, being unwise is different from being ignorant. Unwise people don't do what they know to do; while the ignorant just don't know what to do - yet.

From statistics, we know that over 53% of the people in most of the countries in the Western world don't have any savings at all. About 48% of those on the verge of retirement will have nothing to meet their basic necessities with at retirement!

About 69% of the soon-to-be retirees said they feel guilty about not saving enough.

Riiiiight!!

Forget about the guilt and start doing something about it right now! It is the foolish who know what to do but don't do it!!

As things stand financially with you today, how would you categorise yourself - Wise, unwise or just plain ignorant?

Vision Is Paramount

Whatever your answer is to the question above, I would like you to consider the following statement:

If you can think better, you can see better,
and
if you can see better, you can get better.

It is my opinion that as your way of thinking changes for the better, you will begin to see yourself in a new light: not as you are now but as you desire to be in the future. Brian Tracy said **"All successful people men** and women are big dreamers. They imagine what their future could be, ideal in every respect, and then they work every day toward their distant vision, that goal or purpose".

My coach, Tracy Repchuk, once challenged me that "*instead of just thinking OF your goals, why not begin thinking FROM your goals?*" You may think that is like putting things backwards, right? What she meant was that I needed to begin seeing myself as if my goals had already been accomplished and to conduct myself as such.

The problem is that many people have no vision for their lives at all. You cannot do anything about something you don't *see*. If you are totally blind to it then you cannot do anything about it. When you recognise and acknowledge that there is a problem that needs to be fixed, then you can begin tackling it.

R. Kelly, in his song "**I Believe I Can Fly**", wrote:

> "*If I can **see it**, then I can **do it**
> If I just **believe it,** there's nothing to it
> I believe I can fly
> I believe I can touch the sky*

The Price of Thought-Change

*I **think** about it every night and day*
Spread my wings and fly away
I believe I can soar
*I **see** me running through that open door*
*I **believe** I can fly*
I believe I can fly
I believe I can fly ..."

King Solomon, the wealthiest man who ever lived, said in the Bible, "**Where there is no vision, the people perish...**" (Proverbs 29:18 KJV). Vision shows you what you could be, what you could do and what you could have. Wisdom helps you to devise a plan to make it happen. Discipline enables you to work your way through the difficulties you may encounter. Perseverance helps you to hold on to the vision when the going gets tough.

Once the way you think begins to get transformed, how you see yourself should also change. Don't be like the African Impala, which can jump to a height of over 10 feet and leap a distance of more than 30 feet but yet can be kept in a zoo with a mere 3-foot wall. These magnificent creatures will not jump unless they can see where their feet will fall. This means that African

Impalas will stay trapped in that enclosure because they refuse to jump to where they can't see with their physical eyes!

Many human beings are like those Impalas due to a lack of vision. Some people still embrace the *seeing is believing* notion, but that is like putting the cart before the horse. When it comes to faith in God, the believing and the action come before the seeing. You must see with your mind's eyes first (*vision*) before you can see with your physical eyes (*realisation*).

Be sure to have a vision of what you want to be, to do and to have; then go wholeheartedly after that vision.

****
"If you can dream it, you can do it."
- Walt Disney
****

Yogi Berra said, **"If you don't know where you're going, you probably aren't going to get there."** On the contrary, if you can identify where you want to go in relation to where you are right now, then you are in a good position to also identify the areas of your life that you will need to improve in order for you to arrive at your desired destination.

Vision is a clear, comprehensive, but invisible 'photograph' of a person's life in the future. Your vision is like your desired destination on a map (from where you are currently), and your goals are the little journeys on the road map (with their twists and turns, curves and bends) in between those two points. John Dewey said, **"Arriving at one goal is the starting point to another"**. So getting to your desired destination is like accomplishing a series of goals strung together end-to-end in the direction of your vision.

****

"Vision without action is daydream.
Action without vision is nightmare."
- Japanese Proverb

****

You will need goals if you want to achieve your vision or you will just be like any other 'dreamer' out there who has vision, but no goals to achieve it with. On the other hand, there are those who have lots of goals but no vision! They go from goal to goal without any real purpose. After a while, they give up because there is no great purpose for what they are doing. No Vision; and so there is no desired end of their journey in sight.

Why People Don't Set Goals

As good as goals are, many people do not set any for their lives. I believe one of the reasons why some people don't set goals may be because they don't know what goals are. Some people just assume that their wishes and fantasies are goals. A goal has to be clear, written down, achievable, measurable and time-based. (You should be able to describe your goals to anyone in brief, clear sentences - if asked.)

Worse still, many people have not been exposed to goal-setting and thus don't know it is important. I spent many years in school, college and University; I cannot remember having a minute's lecture dedicated to goalsetting and that may be the same for a lot of people.

The worst reason, in my opinion, why some people don't set goals is that even though they know what goals are, they are afraid they will not be able to accomplish them. So they think that if they don't set goals, they have nothing to mark their miserable lives against or even if they set any goal at all, they set mediocre goals that they can easily achieve; making them live on a level lower than they have been created to live.

From the above, I hope you will agree with me that vision must come before goals. Without it, your goals will mean very little.

Another way to look at vision is seeing it as the trailer of a blockbuster movie featuring the person you are going to be in the near future, but instead of writing **COMING SOON**, you will write **BECOMING SOON**, and then you go out and make that movie come true. By the way, you are the lead actor, producer and director of that movie.

In my book "Milestones of Financial Freedom", I emphasised the need for a 'WHY' (vision) before you focus on the 'WHAT' (goals & objectives) of your financial freedom. Also, in my Money Management Coaching sessions, I always make sure the vision for the future is defined first. I want to create in you a desire to be more than what you are right now, so you can get up and fulfil your true potential. Not only that, many people live in a perpetual cycle of debt all their lives, hoping that one day things will just get better; that might not happen unless you do something about it yourself.

Challenge yourself today to begin thinking differently than before and to begin seeing yourself differently – as you desire to be.

The questions you should answer now are:

- What does the vision of your future-self look like?
- What does that vision say to you and about you?

As your thinking is changing, the words that come out of your mouth will also begin to change. In the next chapter, you will learn when and how to use your speech in the fight for financial freedom.

Chapter 4
The Price of Speech-Change

Most of the time, as individuals, we allow our circumstances and challenges to talk to us, but we don't talk back — even though we should be commanding what we desire into our situations. On the contrary, when it comes to dealing with our fellow human beings, we talk back when we shouldn't. On the road to financial freedom, however, it is necessary that you recognise when to speak up and when to be silent.

The words of our mouths are powerful and creative - if we can only learn to use them aright. The Bible says in Proverbs 18:21 that *"**Death and life are in the power of the tongue, and they who indulge in it shall eat the fruit of it [for death or life].**"* (AMP)

In this chapter, you will learn how to pay the price of financial freedom in both silence and courageous speech. It may seem difficult at first, but you will soon start seeing it pay off as you persist.

One mark of a courageous person is taking responsibility for his or her actions. You don't waste your words to blame events, people, the government or other organisations for your circumstances. If you do, you are giving the power for achieving your financial freedom over to them. *Hold your peace and hold on to your power. Take responsibility and take back control of your own life.* As it's been said, "It is not about the cards you're dealt but how you play those cards that determines whether you win or lose in the game of life".

The mind is a very powerful tool; so is the tongue. If you are not courageous enough, your mind will rule and control you and whatever you say. Have courage; pay the price of speech-change just as you have paid that of thought-change.

Here is how you can do it:

Firstly, begin to speak back to your mind (I can assure you this is not madness).

If you have been in debt for a long time, it is possible that your mind (where your circumstances and challenges are constantly played out to you) will be telling you that things are always going to remain that way. This is an excellent point where you can begin speaking back to your mind - without *losing it,* of course. The only way you can interrupt the constant flow of negative thought running through your mind is to say something positive – out loud.

As a Christian, I read the Bible daily, and it says "... *we have the mind of Christ.*" (1 Corinthians 2:16). I don't think Christ will be telling me that I will forever and ever be a debtor. The mind of Christ stands in sharp contrast to the wisdom of the world; it utilises the wisdom from God and gives believers in Jesus, like me, a special understanding of spiritual matters.

I begin each day by saying what the Bible says about WHO I am, WHAT I have, WHAT I can do and WHAT I can be. You can use your favourite book for these affirmations, but I call myself what God calls me.

This is who I am in Christ:

- I am a child of God - (John 1:12)
- I am a branch of Jesus Christ Who is the True Vine - (John 15:5)

- I am assured that God works for my good in every circumstance - (Romans 8:28)

- I am free from any condemnation brought against me, and I cannot be separated from the love of my God - (Romans 8:31-39)

- I am God's temple - (1 Corinthians 3:16).

- I am a minister of reconciliation for God - (2 Corinthians 5:17-21).

- I am seated with Jesus Christ in heavenly places - (Ephesians 2:6).

- I am confident that God will complete the good work He started in me - (Philippians 1:6).

- I am a citizen of heaven - (Philippians 3:20)

- I am hidden with Christ in God - (Colossians 3:1-4).

- I am born of God, and the evil one cannot touch me - (1 John 5:18).

- I am a believer, and the light of the Gospel shines in my mind (2 Corinthians 4:4).

- I am a doer of the Word, and I am blessed in my actions (James 1:22, 25).

- I am God's workmanship, created in Christ unto good works (Ephesians 2:10).

- I am a new creation in Christ Jesus (2 Corinthians 5:17).

- I am complete in Christ Who is the Head of all principality and power (Colossians 2:10).

- I am alive with Christ (Ephesians 2:5).

- I am free from the law of sin and death (Romans 8:2).

- I am far from oppression, and fear does not come near me (Isaiah 54:14).

- I am holy and blameless before God in love (Ephesians 1:4; 1 Peter 1:16).

- I am a spirit-being; alive to God (Romans 6:11; 1 Thessalonians 5:23).

- I am a joint-heir with Christ (Romans 8:17).

- I am more than a Conqueror through Him Who loves me (Romans 8:37).

- I am an overcomer by the blood of the Lamb and the word of my testimony (Revelation 12:11).

- I am a partaker of God's divine nature (2 Peter 1:3-4).

- I am an ambassador for Christ (2 Corinthians 5:20).

- I am part of a chosen generation, a royal priesthood, a holy nation, a purchased people (1 Peter 2:9).

- I am the righteousness of God in Jesus Christ (2 Corinthians 5:21).

- I am the temple of the Holy Spirit; I am not my own (1 Corinthians 6:19).

- I am the head and not the tail; I am above only and not beneath (Deuteronomy 28:13).

- I am the light of the world (Matthew 5:14).

- I am God's elect, full of mercy, kindness, humility and longsuffering (Romans 8:33; Colossians 3:12).

- I am forgiven of all my sins and washed in the Blood of Jesus (Ephesians 1:7).

- I am delivered from the power of darkness and translated into God's kingdom (Colossians 1:13).

The Price of Speech-Change

- I am redeemed from the curse of sin, sickness, and poverty (Galatians 3:13).

- I am firmly rooted, built up, established in my faith and overflowing with gratitude (Colossians 2:7).

- I am called of God to be the voice of His praise (Psalm 66:8; 2 Timothy 1:9).

- I am healed by the stripes of Jesus (Isaiah 53:5; 1 Peter 2:24).

- I am raised up with Christ and seated in heavenly places (Ephesians 2:6; Colossians 2:12).

- I am greatly loved by God (Romans 1:7; Ephesians 2:4; Colossians 3:12; 1 Thessalonians 1:4).

- I am strengthened with all might according to His glorious power (Colossians 1:11).

- I am submitted to God, and the devil flees from me because I resist him in the Name of Jesus (James 4:7).

- I may approach God with freedom and confidence (Ephesians 3:12)

- I have been chosen and appointed to bear fruit - (John 15:16)

- I have the mind of Christ (1 Corinthians 2:16; Philippians 2:5).

- I have the peace of God that passes all understanding (Philippians 4:7).

- I have been bought with a price and I belong to God - (1 Corinthians 6:19-20)

- I have been established, anointed and sealed by God - (2 Corinthians 1:21-22)

- I have received the gift of righteousness and I reign as a king in life by Jesus Christ (Romans 5:17).

- I have been redeemed and forgiven of all my sins - (Colossians 1:13-14)

- I have received the spirit of wisdom and revelation in the knowledge of Jesus, the eyes of my understanding being enlightened (Ephesians 1:17-18).

- I have given, and it shall be given to me; good measure, pressed down, shaken together, and

The Price of Speech-Change

running over, men shall give into my bosom (Luke 6:38).

- I have the Greater One living in me; greater is He Who is in me than he who is in the world (1 John 4:4).

- I have not been given a spirit of fear but of power, love and a sound mind - (2 Timothy 1:7)

- I have direct access to the throne of grace through Jesus Christ - (Hebrews 4:14-16)

- I have no lack, for my God supplies all of my needs according to His riches in glory by Christ Jesus (Philippians 4:19).

- I can quench all the fiery darts of the wicked one with my shield of faith (Ephesians 6:16).

- I can do all things through Christ Jesus Who strengthens me (Philippians 4:13).

- I press on toward the goal to win the prize to which God in Christ Jesus is calling me upward (Philippians 3:14).

- It is not I who live, but Christ lives in me (Galatians 2:20).

Confessing the above continually will give you both a change in your speech as well as a change in your mind that: you are different; you are special; you can attain any goal; you have Divine help at your disposal, and that everything will be alright.

In the same vein, when things are not going the way you think they should, instead of complaining about your situation, turn it into prayers and ask for God's help. The Bible has this to say in Philippians 4:6-7 (New Living Translation): *"Don't worry about anything; instead, pray about everything. Tell God what you need, and thank him for all he has done. Then you will experience God's peace, which exceeds anything we can understand. His peace will guard your hearts and minds as you live in Christ Jesus."*

Secondly, learn to say 'No' to yourself when it matters.

One of the very first words we learnt to say as children is 'No' – after *da-da,* of course. Why was that? Maybe it was due to the fact that we heard it so frequently, and because it is short and easy to pronounce. 'No' became a more familiar word as we grew from babyhood into toddlerhood. At that stage, we learnt that it was not good manners to say 'No' when you are asked to do something, and we needed to do as we were told.

As children, this was how we learnt to differentiate right from wrong; it was how we learnt which behaviour was acceptable and which ones were not.

As we grow into adulthood, however, we seem to gradually lose the ability to say 'No' in the correct context. It becomes easier to tell our future 'No' than to say 'No' to our immediate desires; so we ignore our budgets and just *go with the flow* and spend money without much thought for the consequences. What we are mostly concerned about is that we please others and release the peer-pressure on us; thereby ultimately displeasing ourselves and our financial future or freedom.

If you have got yourself into a financial pit by trying to please others or by comparing yourself to them, then it is time to start saying 'No' to yourself again on spending or a lifestyle that will keep you in a perpetual debt cycle.

You, the impulsive spender, should try this little exercise the next time you are tempted to buy on impulse:

> *When your eyes focus on an item that is not in your plan (or budget) and your mind agrees to the sudden "need" for that item, let your mouth say 'No' so that your ears and the rest of your body can hear you. Then shift your gaze from the item and walk away.*

That may sound funny, but learning to say 'No' to things you don't need means you are able to say 'Yes' to things you do desire, which, in this case, is your financial freedom.

On the opposite end of the 'speaking out' spectrum is "knowing NOT to talk back" when people criticise you as you go along your journey to Financial Freedom.

An old children's rhyme goes like this:

> *"Sticks and stones*
> *may break my bones*
> *but words will never hurt me."*

Words will never hurt you?! What planet are you from?!!

Whoever wrote that rhyme has never been hurt by words, especially when they come from close friends or relatives.

Sometimes, even those who know next to nothing about your life will criticise you. They will say you are dreaming for thinking that the grass is greener on the other side, even though they themselves have never ventured beyond their front yard! If, however, you see your critics for what they really are, you might begin developing immunity to their comments.

****

> *"Those who have done nothing in life are not qualified to judge those who have done little."*
> *- Samuel Johnson*

****

By definition, a *critic* is someone who makes negative judgements or predictions about other people. Critics are not interested in helping anyone improve; but rather enjoy seeing others fail so they can say their negative predictions came true after all. Critics are often jealous of your talents, or your proposed destination in business, career or in life. Most of the time, they have never been and may never get to where you are aiming for.

You have three choices on how to respond to your critics:

1. **Ignore your critics** - ignoring someone or something means your attention is on something else, something better for you.

   "When those who don't know how you're going to end up make a mockery of you, ignore them. Don't pay attention to those who don't know what you know." - Brooklyns Ovie

2. **Be inspired by your critics** - Use the criticism as inspiration to succeed. Use their hurtful words as stepping stones towards your financial freedom. Concentrate on the results you are aiming for, and as they say, *"results take away insults"*.

3. **Agree with your critics** - if you allow someone who has not accomplished something close to what you are aiming for to talk you into giving up, then you are not really ready for financial freedom. They have, in turn,

succeeded in derailing you off your path. Misery, they say, loves company.

At the crucifixion of Jesus, after He had been nailed to the cross (Matthew 27:39-44), almost everyone was making fun of Him. Not only the common folks but the elders, scribes and Pharisees as well but in all of that, He kept quiet.

Why?

That was part of the price He had to pay for our salvation. When it was necessary for Him to speak, He spoke words so important that they had to be recorded. He even got one poor fellow on the cross beside Him an *entry pass* into Paradise that day!

When you are trying to become financially free, you will inevitably hear comments and all sorts of negative 'advice'. If you, however, try to acknowledge everyone for what they are saying to you, you will lose focus of your mission. The best thing you can do is to keep quiet, remain focused and keep going on your way to financial freedom.

The results of your actions, in the long run, will speak for you. I believe this is a price worth paying.

The Price of Financial Freedom

Chapter 5
The Price of Facing Oppositions

If you are going to accomplish anything worthwhile in life, don't be surprised at the opposition you will encounter – expect it! What you will not know right away is where the opposition will come from – within or without.

The price of financial freedom is much less or not very evident for those who know how to live frugally and are content with a moderate standard of living. They can become just as free, by adopting a frugal lifestyle, as people who have (or have displayed) a great deal of affluence.

For people who have been living as though there is no tomorrow and have suddenly decided that they want to change their family tree financially, the changes may look drastic and will definitely be more evident to people around them. This is where the oppositions begin.

Opposition from Your 'OLD' Self

The first opposition will come from your own self – your body. Can you remember how your body used to go into *survival mode* the moment you declared that you would be fasting or going on a diet? A similar thing is going to happen here when you declare frugality in your spending – be prepared.

Your former-self may have been in financial bondage for many years and has become accustomed to it. Your body is going to react to the idea of becoming financially-free because the *status quo* is about to change. The changes will come in these ways:

1. **Comfort.** This is one of those things that some people just "can't" live without, but most can. It is often the first thing to be shed off when you are seeking financial freedom. Examining your life and determining what you have to *do without* is not very comfortable for anyone. Giving up on buying a newer car, going on "staycations" instead of vacations, eating menus based on beans & rice instead of a steak barbeque with friends are things you have to get used to, but your body (and pride) will oppose you. The

question is: how much comfort are you willing to give up for your financial freedom?

2. Achieving your financial freedom is going to take a lot of **hard work and energy**. It means exerting yourself physically; whether you work on a rooftop in construction or in an office, you're moving around all day long. It means exerting yourself mentally, stressing and worrying over projects and interpersonal relationships. It means exerting yourself emotionally, investing in yourself, your life, other people, or products.

Maybe you have realised that you need to earn more money to achieve your goals; let's say you need about £200 more a month to throw at your debt, or you just need a few more hundreds to clear a certain loan or credit card, you may take a second job; you may write articles for a money-making blog in the mornings before going to work, you may do bookkeeping for freelancers at weekends; you end each day more exhausted than the last, but you tell yourself that it is worth it, because soon enough you won't have to do as much anymore.

3. Due to your newfound money-making activities, **your time** for other things is going to be reduced. The questions you must have definite answers for are: how many days will you have to work, slave or grind through in order to find financial peace? How much of your life is going to be used up trying to achieve your goals? Will it be worth it in the end?

In his book "<u>The Battle is the Lord's</u>", Owen C. Carr related how his father reacted to the news that he was going into the ministry. His father told him, **'If you're going to start, don't stop. And if you're going to stop, don't start.'** The same is true of Financial Freedom. You either get ready to pay the price wholeheartedly or go back to your *comfortable*, debt-ridden, underachieving life.

Opposition from Family

I have listened to many call-in radio programs in my time and one thing I have noticed is that when a family is in financial trouble, only one person calls in for help, but when they become debt-free, everybody joins in on the shout of victory.

When you, as an individual, have decided to conquer your 'personal' oppositions as detailed above, and it is time to introduce the new 'regime' to the family, don't be surprised if you are met with strong opposition as well. You would be treated as if you had suddenly contracted a disease called MFTIACS – 'My Family Thinks I Am Crazy Syndrome'.

The mistake many heads of families make is to tell the family HOW they are going to achieve financial freedom instead of first informing them of the reasons WHY. Tell them the 'why' and the benefits in the long run; paint a good picture of what the future can be; when everyone understands that, then the 'how' can follow.

Opposition from Friends

There are friends and *there are friends*. If you are waiting for applause from all your friends for your attempt at financial freedom, you will wait for a long time. Some of your friends will think you have gone crazy when you begin with your efforts to become financially free.

The Price of Financial Freedom

Your social life may become non-existent because you will now be unwilling to unnecessarily waste the endless hours it takes to maintain the scores of friendships and acquaintances craved by the insecure. That's the truth.

Your friends will not understand you unless they have had the same thought-change. They will not understand why you are not willing to waste time chatting, drinking, discussing tabloid newspaper stories and watching soap operas.

In the worst-case scenario, you may even lose some of your friends who don't want to identify with your debt-free life, even though they want the same end result. When you become financially free, it may be too difficult for some of your friends to cope with having you around them because the implication is that they too could get the same result, and that would mean work and effort. That's bad news for them. They'd rather avoid you or talk you down than be faced with your silent *'accusation'* every time they see you.

The Price of Facing Oppositions

Opposition from The Government

Being financially free sometimes brings a different kind of opposition from the government. Even though governments may like jobs to be created, they don't seem to like the people who create them and are NOT in debt.

They seem to loathe wealthy people because wealth brings personal power and individual freedom. Some governments do not like it if a "mindless" worker acquires personal power. They prefer *faceless production units*, as someone puts it, hovering in a no-man's land of the false hope of an *everlasting pension*; kept just above the absolute poverty line by taxation.

The tax burden is carefully calculated to stop just short of causing people to riot in the streets. It is designed to allow people to have some small hope of dragging themselves out of debt one day, or being able to pay their bills.

They do not like strong-minded, wealth-creating individualists. Some governments seem to operate through the tyranny of the majority. Whatever people clamour for, that's what is given, and most people these days are shouting "tax the rich to feed the poor!".

What these people don't realise is that, on the universal scale of things, the rich actually pay less taxes than the poor – no matter what the government tells you!

Opposition from Strangers

When you have control of your finances, almost the entire world could be against you. Most people will consider you 'lucky' to have made some wealth. To them, wealth creation is a purely random event which happens accidentally *to* someone with no effort on their part at all.

These are people who spend their lives sitting around waiting for this *miracle* to happen to them. When it happens to you, and you get 'lucky' (after ten or twenty years of back-breaking effort), they become jealous.

Don't be surprised also if these strangers stretch out their hands in an attempt to claim 'their' share of your money. You may be treated like those lottery winners who suddenly began getting thousands of letters. from long-lost *'relatives',* requesting money. Failure to comply will be met with public clamour of 'Miser' before you know it.

Are you willing to overcome all these oppositions for the sake of becoming financially free or not?

Financial freedom is a choice, and it is also your responsibility as you drag your family away from perpetual debt. No one can make the choice for you, and no one will pay the price for you.

Chapter 6
Learn to Play the Game of Life

Brian Tracy said, **"Life is not a rehearsal for something else; this is the only one you've got"**. To which I will add "on this earth anyway".

Truth be told, the older you get, the more conscious you will become about your age AND your status in life. This is the point when you may begin to question your life choices, and asking yourself what kind of game you have been playing so far with your life.

This life has been called many things by many people: a journey; a dream, a highway; a teacher, a gift; a test; a one-time offer; a story; a song; a play; a work in progress; a challenge, a duty, a battle; an adventure, etc. But the one I like to use most is that **life is a game**.

If life is really a game, who are the players? Who is the umpire and what are the rules?

As long as we are alive, we are all players in the game of life, whether we know it or not. This reminds me of

Christopher McDougall's saying that **"Every morning in Africa, a gazelle wakes up and it knows it must run faster than the fastest lion or it will be killed. Every morning, a lion wakes up in Africa, and it knows it must outrun the slowest gazelle or it will starve to death. It doesn't matter whether you're a lion or a gazelle. When the sun comes up, you'd better be running."**

This book you are holding is written with you, as an individual, in mind. The whole world may be heading in one direction, but since you are a unique creation of God, should you be heading the same way without a reason?

What some people call a game is actually a survival issue for others. Life will push you in the direction it wants you to go; make you think certain thoughts about yourself; cause you to make some utterances about your situation and even send opposition your way - just for fun! If you are going to win at this game, you have to push back – hard. You are not a dead fish that is floating down the river; you are a living, breathing and forward-looking individual who swims against the current in order to win.

Look around you and you will notice that almost everyone seems to be running – just like the lion and the gazelle you read about earlier. The problem is that most people are just running because that is what they have been taught to do; they don't know why they are doing it. They are not sure if they are running from something or running after something else. At least the African lion and the gazelle in the jungle have their reasons for running.

****

"The major quest in life is not what you are getting but what you are becoming."
- Dave Ramsey

****

Is it not time for us to stop, take stock of our lives and find out what we are really running from or towards? To do this, you must ask yourself these critical questions:

- Are you the lion or the gazelle?
- Are you the chaser or the chased?
- Can the roles be reversed?
- If so, which one would you like to be?

The answers you give to these questions will dictate how you apply your time and efforts in your daily activities. In doing so, you will have a daily focus and a yardstick for measuring your progress instead of remaining in the camp of those whose motto, after their daily aimless running, is 'tomorrow is another day'.

Someone once said, **"Life is a boomerang; what you give, you get back"** - in abundance. The main rule in the game of life can be found in Genesis 8:22 in the Bible, which says: *"While the earth remains, seedtime and harvest, cold and heat, winter and summer, and day and night shall not cease."* What that means is that what you put into life is what you get back in multiple times. You will reap what you sow. If you put in nothing, you get nothing back. But if you put time and effort into what you desire, you will get great results back. Seasons will change unfailingly, but you will only have something good to reap if you have sown the seed for it beforehand.

In order to win at the game of life, you need to begin thinking about *growth*. Put time and effort into what you want back on your way to financial freedom. Be consistently progressive and develop a growth mindset.

A growth mindset is not intimidated by mistakes and setbacks because it sees them as learning opportunities. Someone with a growth mind-set does not entertain fear because they know that, in learning something new, mistakes are bound to happen. But instead of focusing on the mistakes or on being perfect, you must focus on improving yourself and making progress.

The African lion may head a pride with many *hunters* to choose from; but he does not give up hunting just because the pride lost a *game (or prey)*. They re-group and go hunting again and again – using different tactics to succeed each time.

To make a start in any venture, you have to take a step first. If you hit a roadblock in your quest for financial freedom, don't give up. Analyse your situation from all possible angles; then choose the best solution to get you moving again. Whatever happens, don't give up.

Robert Strauss said, **"Success is like wrestling a gorilla. You don't quit when you're tired. You quit when the gorilla is tired."** The gazelle that wants to stay alive will not regard its tired legs. It will *bob and weave* until the lion gives up on chasing him. This is how to play the game of life.

Truth be told, there are people who are 'ruthless' in the way they play any game. They are prepared to win at all costs. They neither show fear nor mercy; everyone else is fair game; they will bend the rules wherever possible and cheat if they get the opportunity. You know people like that, don't you?

We, however, are not gazelles, lions or gorillas who just follow their animalistic instincts and have no moral consciousness. We should not leave our fellow humans hurt, bruised, battered, wounded and dead in our wake just because we want to make it in life. The Bible says in Ecclesiastes 9:11, *"I returned and saw under the sun that—The race is not to the swift, nor the battle to the strong, nor bread to the wise, nor riches to men of understanding, nor favour to men of skill; but time and chance happen to them all."* (NKJV). The best players in this game are usually those who carry others along in their success.

Did you realise that when the game ends, everything goes back into the 'box' – including your body? At the end of your life, what will you show for it? The people you have helped or those you have hurt? Will you reach the top of the ladder only to find it leaning against the wrong wall?

The owner of your life will demand an account of how you used it. Make sure you are running with the right objective in mind and for the right prize.

Chapter 7
The Prize of Change

From the earlier chapters, we know that financial freedom is costly (mentally and emotionally, to say the least) and the price is always paid in advance. No exceptions. Your efforts to become financially free will change you in a lot of ways. I hope I've been able to convince you that this freedom will cause you to:

- Think differently
- Speak differently
- See yourself differently
- Perform tasks differently
- Pray and read scriptures differently
- Become disciplined
- Become committed to your goals and dreams
- Use time and resources wisely

- Forgo some sleep time (getting up earlier or sleeping later) for a while

- Admit you don't know it all and get help

- Take some classes and/or get a coach

- And much more

I'm sure you would also agree with me that this is not an exhaustive list; nevertheless, what you have learnt so far could create a huge change in you. Les Brown, said **"To achieve something you've never achieved before, you must become someone you've never been before"**.

After paying the necessary price for financial freedom, surely there has to be a *'pot of gold waiting for you at the end of the rainbow'*. Shouldn't it?

Yes, there is a reward for all your hard work, which might take a few months or even years, but it will be worth it in the long run. Here are some of them:

1. **Debt Free Living.**

    Financial freedom and debt are arch-enemies; it is difficult to have both at the same time. The elimination of your debt leads the way to financial freedom. A person with debt is not yet financially free because, in a sense, he or she is still a servant to at least one lender. People with debt are required to meet the terms of their debt repayment rather than using their money however they please or how God wants them to. They are not truly free until they learn how to eliminate debt from their lives.

Being financially free means you have passed the stage of just being debt-free, and you can continue living that way. You are free to spend money wisely and at the same time, free from the bondage of debt.

2. **Stress-Free Living**.

Your relationships will no longer be affected by stress brought on by money problems. Even your health will improve with your newfound peace of mind. Do you know how many people have forgotten how life used to be before heavy debts took over their lives? YOU will be free to live in peace again.

3. **Wealth-Building Becomes Easier.**

   Without debt repayments, you now have complete control of your most powerful wealth-building tool – your income. Freedom is a condition under which wealth can be created and increased easily. Freedom is needed to exploit ideas intelligently; freedom to take calculated risks (e.g. starting new businesses). Freedom to do a job you like and enjoy, rather than one you just endure.

4. **New View Of Work And Retirement**

   If you enjoy your job and have money to do what you want to do now and in the future, you can consider yourself financially free even while you are working for the government or a company. Some people may opt for an early retirement from their main career and work part-time at something they enjoy during some of their retirement years. This is also a way to experience financial freedom.

5. **Change in Your Family Tree.**

   When you are financially free, have made sensible investments, and you are earning enough passive income from them so that you never have to necessarily work to survive, your offsprings will realise that being in debt is NOT the way to live. Their mentality about money and wealth will be different from that of the world that is drowning in debt. Thus, your family gets changed by learning that dependence on debt is folly.

6. **Freedom to Serve God by Helping Others.**

   Jesus said in the Bible that "*No one can serve two masters*" (Matthew 6:24). You cannot serve God and your lenders at the same time. Do you think they call that plastic *Master*Card for nothing?

   Once you have taken care of the present (no more debt) and retirement (your family is taken care of), it is now time to have fun (with your giving) in a new way - *helping others as God intends*. You will enjoy it. Without any payments, you can serve God as you are originally meant to; and with the freedom to volunteer your time and expertise as well.

What's more? Lots. If you can dream it, the sky is the limit to what you can be, do, and have. You are free to dream more clearly as your investments are feeding you instead of your debts eating you up alive.

Now that things are looking up for you, don't look back. Robert Kiyosaki said, **"You're only poor if you give up. The most important thing is that you did something. Most people only talk and dream of getting rich. You've done something."** To which I will add **"Don't stop now, you're doing so well"**.

Chapter 8
And Finally ...

The simple fact that you know what price you are going to pay for financial freedom does not mean it will be easy. *Simple* does not mean *easy,* but if your mind is made up, you will use obstacles as stepping stones and not tombstones.

****

"If you do what is easy your life will be hard but if you do what is hard your life will be easy!"
- Les Brown

****

Please note that the prices mentioned in this book may not be the only ones you have to pay for your freedom; they are just the major ones I paid for mine. I hope, however, that I have been able to convince you that just working hard alone does not *cut it* anymore and that you must have a dream and a plan to make that dream come to pass. The dream must be the finished future you desire to have. Mind you, it could involve a lot of determination as you work to overcome some challenges you will face in the form of setbacks and disappointments.

I have written this book to provoke you into doing something about your finances, but that does not mean you should not be thankful for your current situation. You should be thankful in every circumstance you find yourself. You should be thankful that you picked up this book that's provoking you. You should be thankful that you still have time to correct your financial mistakes. Be thankful, but make a move. Don't hate your situation to the extent that you will sit down in disgust and do nothing about it. The Bible says in Philippians 4:6, ***"Don't worry about anything; instead, pray about everything. Tell God what you need, and thank him for all he has done."*** (NLT).

Thank God that you have the opportunity to move ahead. You should give thanks whether things are going well or not; at least you still have the chance to make amends. Our God is a God of second chances. The only question is, 'Are you going to take the opportunity that you have been presented with?'

And Finally ...

Challenges are a part of success. You must learn to make the seemingly uncomfortable activities become comfortable and to make self-discipline your best friend in order to realise your dreams. Let nothing deter you. The obstacles you will encounter may actually *appear* worse in your mind than it is in reality.

Overcome your first challenge – begin today to move towards your financial freedom. Making that effort builds something on the inside of you that, when you overcome one challenge, you are prepared to face the next one because you now have momentum.

****

*"Happy are those who dream dreams
and are willing to pay the price to
make them come true."
– Unknown*

****

Remember that financial freedom won't just come to you. No amount of wishing will make that happen. You have to be hungry for it and be willing to go after it wholeheartedly. That means getting up and going to work. If you can't find any work, create one. Use all the resources that you have been endowed with to make something good of yourself. Turn the television off; stop wasting time watching those who can't sing, can't dance, can't act on 'talent' or 'reality' shows and make better use of *your* talent and time.

Truth be told, it is not as if one can place a monetary value on this thing called freedom; if we could, it would be worth every penny. Ask anyone who has ever been held captive for ransom, and in the face of death, all earthly riches seemed like nothing, hardly worth a thought, when compared to the notion of death or never, ever being free again. So why would you stay in financial bondage?

You have read a lot in this book; you've learnt about choices and sacrifices to be made, and commitments to be adhered to. Those are the things that separate winners from losers. If it were easy, everyone would do it. For you, it is time to stop being the same person you used to be and doing the same things you used to do. It is time to change. Change your thinking, change your talking, and change your attitude, change your actions.

And Finally ...

****

"The act of taking the first step is what separates the winners from the losers."
- Brian Tracy

****

The starting point of all achievement is desire. Would you pay the price that it would take to be financially free?

I will leave you with an adaptation of a 1916 poem by Berton Braley that I once heard Les Brown, the motivational speaker, recite. I hope it will motivate you to willingly and fully pay the price for your financial freedom.

Success

"If you want a thing bad enough
To go out and fight for it,
To work day and night for it,
To give up your time, your peace, and your sleep for it
. . .
If all that you dream and scheme is about it,
And life seems useless and worthless without it . . .

The Price of Financial Freedom

*If you'll gladly sweat for it
And fret for it
And plan for it
And lose all your terror of the opposition for it . . .*

*If you'll simply go after that thing that you want
With all of your capacity,
Strength and sagacity,
Faith, hope and confidence and stern pertinacity . . .*

*If neither cold, poverty, famine nor gaunt,
Sickness nor pain of body and brain,
Can keep you away from the thing that you want . . .*

*If dogged and grim you besiege and beset it,
With the help of God, you WILL get it!"*

Financial Freedom Series

The Price of Financial Freedom is the second book in Niyi's Financial Freedom Series which is an education in not just how to earn money, but to know what it means to you and how to take the unbeaten path to your financial freedom.

The other books in the series are: "Milestones of Financial Freedom" and "Winning Together".

You can get your copies on Amazon website.

Financial Freedom Series

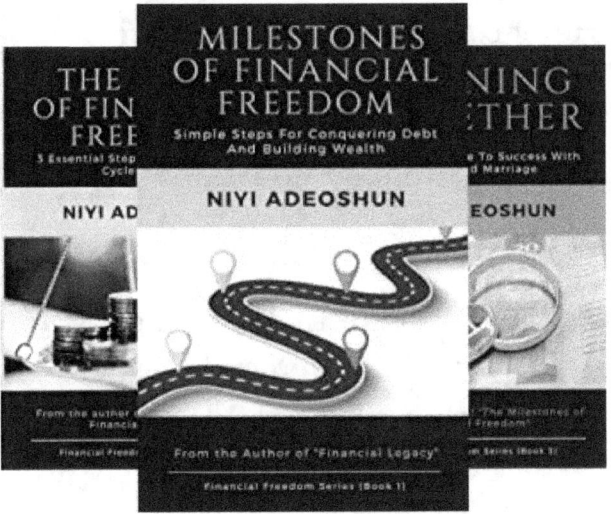

Available in paperback and Kindle

About The Author

Niyi Adeoshun, the Money Management Coach, has been involved in developing financial software for Banks, Insurance and Mortgage companies for over two decades. He, however, specialises in inspiring and motivating people to live a life of financial-freedom in order to fulfil their God-given life purposes.

Niyi, who is a Budget Coach to many individuals and families, has spoken to audiences of various sizes and classes. He encourages the subscribers to his Money Management Tips newsletter on a regular basis via email. He uses his YouTube channels to answer various personal finance questions from viewers all over the world.

His books on personal finance like "Milestones of Financial Freedom", "Financial Legacy" have, for many years, been a blessing to people all over the world and testimonies are still coming in as to how they are impacting lives for the better.

Niyi lives with his family in Essex, UK.

Other Books by the Author

If you have enjoyed this book, you may want to check out other books by the author.

Milestones of Financial Freedom
Simples Steps for Conquering Debt and Building Wealth.

Winning Together
A Couple's Guide to Success with Money and Marriage

Job Loss, Not Life Loss
A Step-by-Step Guide to Emotional, Financial, and Career Recovery

Lies We Believe about Money
Why Christians Struggle with Wealth—and What God Says About It

Financial Legacy
8 Lessons My Father Taught Me about Money

Joshua, Jordan, and Jericho
Reaching Beyond All Obstacles to Your Destiny

The Worship Minister
Pleasing God as We Fulfil His Call

Worship: The God Experience
Engaging With The Presence of God Constantly

Resources

One of the most widely known things that Niyi does is his email newsletter, called Money Management Tips. Anyone can subscribe by visiting his website. If you subscribe today, there is a special gift waiting for you there: http://www.niyiadeoshun.com

Niyi loves doing public speaking, be it in a school, college, church or other Christian organisations. His talks are a blend of motivation, humour and common sense using biblical principles. He always challenges his audiences to aim for success through growth in all areas if life. People are informed, educated and somehow entertained. To have Niyi speak to your church, group or function, contact him at: info@niyiadeoshun.com

Niyi guides individuals and families on debt elimination and total financial freedom strategies. He loves working with people who are determined to fulfil their goals and create the life they really want! It is eye-opening, and wonderful things happen!

You can connect with Niyi through these avenues:
Website: http://www.niyiadeoshun.com/
Email: info@niyiadeoshun.com
Twitter: https://twitter.com/niyiadeoshun
Facebook: https://www.facebook.com/MoneyManagementCoach
YouTube Channel: https://www.youtube.com/c/NiyiAdeoshun

www.ingramcontent.com/pod-product-compliance
Lightning Source LLC
Chambersburg PA
CBHW052327220526
45472CB00001B/308